THE JOY OF HEAVEN 2

The Journey Continues

Advantage
BOOKS
www.advbookstore.com

Written and Illustrated by
Daniel Leske

"…they shall MOUNT up with wings as eagles…" Isaiah 40:31

The Joy of Heaven 2: The Journey Continues by Daniel Leske

Copyright © 2014 by Daniel Leske

All Rights Reserved.

ISBN: 978-1-59755-242-4

Published by: ADVANTAGE BOOKS™
Longwood, Florida, USA
www.advbookstore.com

Library of Congress Catalog Number: 2014951371

First Printing: October 2014
14 15 16 17 18 19 20   10 9 8 7 6 5 4 3 2 1
Printed in the United States of America

By writing this book, I knew the Lord had to open the door into heaven for this story to be written! As you read it, I believe that you'll be inspired by the beauty of heaven and the specialness to it!

Wings are a very special part of heaven!

Felicia is about 8 or 9 years old in stature and Wee Angel is diminutive, like her name.

I tried to paint a picture so that you can envision it!

Each person may see and feel the experience differently. As the writer, I feel that I accomplished what I set out to do!

Always remember that the Lord is the guide.

Now go with me through that doorway ------ the doorway into heaven. I hope you enjoy the story!

Daniel Leske

List of Some of the Characters

Wee Angel	She has white hair and is always a little smaller than any other angels.
Felicia	She is about 8 or 9 years old in stature with blonde hair.
Sir William	A special white winged horse.
Tuddley Teddy	A brown bear that is a friend to everyone.
Lord God Almighty	He rules heaven and earth from his throne in heaven.
Jesus	The Only Begotten Son of God.
Annie.	A tall cougar with wings.
Angel Heather	A angel guide to mansions.
Angel Michelle	A special angel at one of the mansions.
Longstreet	A smaller white buffalo.
April and Hope	Two parrots.

Also a congregation of saints and angels, animals and birds that are all a part of the Lord's kingdom.

Chapter 1

The Arrival

As the heavenly day was awesome, Wee Angel and Felicia were waiting on the heavenly lands outside of the hills that made up the open sanctuary. Felicia was still, with so much in her heart over everything she had seen there!

Her emotions ran deep as her heavenly soul poured out with love after seeing the service.

Wee Angel was also quiet, because she knew that the service did this to those that were new to heaven and the graces of it.

Others walked out on various paths that headed to other heavenly destinations. They were on the other side of the sanctuary from before the service and knew Sir William would soon be there.

Soon they saw him flying in the sky, coming closer to them. He saw them and landed near them.

The glories of the skies were beaming! It was so beautiful!

Felicia had a tear of joy come forth. Others passed by them: some praising God, some joyfully laughing and smiling, others in tears, expressing the moment.

Various animals grazed in the distance along with some horses that were to be ridden if needed by anyone. There were both horses and winged horses.

Sir William walked up to Wee Angel and Felicia and put his head by them so they could hug him.

"Sir William, it was so beautiful!" spoke Felicia.

"I knew you would love it so much!" added Wee Angel. "It won't be the last time, this is heaven!" continued Wee Angel. "This is heaven! It always is! Know that Felicia!"

Felicia was now wearing a lavender colored robed garment as Wee Angels was more light green in color!

They had come out of the sanctuary on a golden pathway through some hills that surrounded it. These actually helped make up the sanctuary area. They were in the heavenly lands, that were open with areas of flowers and grazing areas for the animals. A distance away was a grouping of oak trees and cedar trees for those coming and going to the sanctuary.

Above a flock of white doves flew past them. Other birds sang in the trees. They saw in the distance, a waterfall, hilly areas, and mountains. In between were fields of flowers with golden paths.

There were benches placed in special areas along the golden walkways. Each area had the most beautiful flowers and bushes. These flowers with vines were a lot like the morning glory flowers on earth. There was rich grass everywhere.

Both talked and were grooming Sir William.

They looked out and away from the sanctuary to the heavenly skies.

Wee Angel said to Felicia, "Look what's coming? Look at that!"

Both their eyes were very wide open at what they viewed!

At this time, a few saints, came pass them from the worship and singing service.

Even, Sir William glanced and looked at the riders that were approaching them.

There were some roses by a flowered bench nearby them.

Wee Angel flew and got some of them. No thorns, of course, and she gave some to Felicia.

"Hold on to these, Felicia. You'll need them for what's going to happen!" Wee Angel explained.

Each had ten roses of various colors like the rainbow!

Both Wee Angel and Felicia were amazed as they looked at this brightness of light around them. Beaming glories!

"Oh how bright it is!" whispered Felicia.

Sir William already knew what was going to happen as he whinnied a mighty sound that filled the heavenly air.

Everyone within hearing looked at him. All were always awed by his beauty, for they knew he was a very special horse. It was the sound of a trumpet, but in horse language.

It was the first time Felicia had heard this from Sir William.

"My!" she said, "Oh my! What a powerful sound from Sir William."

"You'll know what it's about pretty soon, Felicia!" Wee Angel said as she flew around Sir William and Felicia with joyful sounds coming from her mouth as well!

The heavenly air seemed filled with praises in the spirit!

Everything seemed to show high glory.

The heavenly air was alive and getting more alive over the moment.

A flock of doves and pigeons flew past them. Song sparrows were busy singing! Robins, finches, and others as well!

The riders were getting closer.

Felicia saw now that they were all on white horses as they flew over the heavenly lands towards them.

There were about twenty to thirty riders on the horses.

Wee Angel and Felicia flew about, both with roses in their hands, waited for something special to happen!

Chapter 2

The Riders

The winged horses with riders gently landed on the open grass by the sanctuary. Both Wee Angel and Felicia stood and stayed where they were until all had landed there. The riders were dressed in garments of oft white in color.

Wee Angel knew who they were and said, "Felicia, I'm not to say a lot yet! But know these are special riders and they came here for a reason."

"My!" said Felicia, "I'm so awed, and they seem powerful. There's something so powerful about them."

"I know Felicia." added Wee Angel, "Just wait! You'll know more!"

One rider, who as he stood, commanded the others in a language Felicia didn't know!

"He's the leader." whispered Wee Angel.

The area was filled with tremendous light yet soft and very powerful, especially around the horses and the riders. The riders were all dressed in special suits. They were suits of protection if needed!

All of this was hard on Felicia's eyes, as the brightness was so great!

"Felicia, remember what I told you." explained Wee Angel, "That in heaven, the light could be so great that you couldn't look at it with earthly eyes! Now

Felicia, you're showing signs of the light being hard on your heavenly eyes. Just know this light is extremely bright with power as willed! These riders and horses, right now, are at a low energy but that can change quickly if needed!"

The riders talked to each other, yet they noticed little Felicia and Wee Angel. They spoke to their horses and the horses all nodded together to Wee Angel, Felicia and Sir William.

Sir William whose being was brighter than ever as he stood, and he knew the horses as well as the riders.

At this time, Wee Angel and Felicia looked up above the sanctuary grounds. A group of angels flew above with trumpets, and sounded a mighty sound. Glories filled the air!

Then many angels flew above everyone. They hovered and sang praises. More trumpet sounds filled the heavenly air. The golden path from the sanctuary was all light and very bright, yet through some of the hills walked Jesus with an angel.

All his riders knelt in honor of him. Wee Angel and Felicia did the same.

Jesus nodded to the leader and then his face turned towards Wee Angel, Felicia and Sir William. Jesus was in a robe of royalty. His garment was fine linen, very white, yet so pleasing to the eyes. On his shoulders he had a special purple extra outer garment. Three gems on each shoulder that emitted powerful beams of light. The robes, themselves were of light, making them so appealing to their eyes. It was as though the garments kept in the light so that the light was not so powerful and others could see him and not so much radiance.

His face was the brightness of light and his eyes, they glowed with soft blues radiated by the gold and golden tones of light about his face.

As Felicia looked at his hair, she saw the browns, yet golden and interesting like the colors of the rainbow at the edges, because of the light surrounding him.

Four angels came flying over areas of flowers. There were dahlia's, hyacinths, even daffodils as well as others. Then they flew next to Sir William, Wee Angel, and Felicia.

There was sereneness to everything.

The flowers breathed the sereneness!

The birds breathed it!

The angels breathed it!

The riders breathed it!

The horses breathed it!

Everything seemed to know and breathe with this presence of Jesus!

Felicia and Wee Angel could not even talk if they wanted too!

The moment was special! The glories of heaven were so real!

Felicia and Wee Angel still stood holding the roses.

Chapter 3

Jesus and Riders

The riders with Jesus stood and waited to leave the sanctuary grounds. Their apparel was robe-like in appearance and cut, yet different from others that Wee Angel and Felicia had passed or seen, including the angels such as Michael.

Their attire was with shirts and pants, yet they had a coat-like half robe over the top of this.

The half robe had buttons on the half sleeves. They again were pure gems. Some had five of them on each sleeve. Others a lesser amount, each had different colors, but all gems on each rider's garment were the same color, with lights beaming from them. Pure reds, pure greens, pure blues, pure lavenders, pure burgundies were the colors. The gem lights were round, yet shaped and fairly large in size.

The shoulders had a special pad on them with golden pieces that looked like clips. Again in the center of each clip were real small gems, but clear in color, with beams of bright white light coming through them. All the riders had the same.

Their slacks were loosely fitted, but just right for flight on the horses. Their boots were special browns with golden hues and golden pieces placed in locations on the boots. These were golden lights! They also had on special belts, golden in tones, with smaller gems, with light that came from them.

These winged horses had special saddles (as we call them), not overly done! Pleasing in silvery colors, with gems of amber and bright silver pieces with amber colored gems.

These were the clothes of the riders.

Jesus nodded to Felicia and Wee Angel, "My children, come here."

They ran carrying their roses and handed them to Jesus.

Felicia had tears in her eyes and Wee Angel, bowed her head! Jesus took the roses from them and picked each one up and hugged them.

"Jesus, we love you!" both said together in teared, broken, and sweet voices. Jesus introduced Angel Micah to Felicia and more hugs! Jesus thanked them for the roses and gave them to the leader of the riders.

Jesus spoke, "Felicia, Wee Angel! Is it possible I could use (----------) awhile?

"Yes, Jesus absolutely." Wee Angel answered.

Felicia was perplexed as she didn't understand what Jesus called Sir William.

Jesus and Sir William walked away to an open area.

"I didn't understand what Jesus called Sir William." Felicia said.

Wee Angel answered, "Jesus has a special name for Sir William. We'll talk about it at another time. This is his horse when he goes riding, but Jesus wants others to see him too!"

Sir William had already placed his head by Jesus.

Jesus turned and said, "Wee Angel! Felicia! We are going for just a nice ride. You'll have him later, again. I love both of you."

Angel Micah stood by Wee Angel and Felicia .

The light around Jesus and Sir William grew stronger and very bright! They couldn't even be seen because of its brightness, then the light lessened and they saw Jesus in his new apparel.

He was dressed like the others, only on his sleeves were three rows of gems with twelve in all on each sleeve.

With very bright golden light coming forth. The most beautiful color golden, different from everyone else.

His hair was proper for the ride. About his head were rows, crown-like golden lights that encircled his head, signifying his leadership and authority. Sir William now had on a special saddle, like the others, but just a little nicer.

As Jesus was doing this, the leader of the riders had gotten them all in a straight line, back on their winged horses and ready for flight!

They nodded to Jesus who was now on the back of Sir William. Then in orderly fashion the horses opened their wings and at command began to wing their way upwards into the heavenly sky.

What power filled the heavenly sky as well as the awesome light colors coming from the gems.

"My Wee Angel, what a sight to see!" said Felicia.

More tears of joy from Felicia.

"This is heaven, there is so much to see and be apart of!" said Wee Angel.

Angel Micah said his good days to Wee Angel and Felicia, then he too was in the heavenly sky back to the Lord's city.

Both stood and watched and watched and watched! The horses flew off to the horizon over the fields of flowers, golden ways, streams, trees, and other heavenly land.

They both prayed.

Wee Angel softly spoke, "Thank you, Jesus! Thank you!"

They had heavy hearts of joy. The joy of heaven!

Daniel Leske

Chapter 4

They Meet Him Again

Both Wee Angel and Felicia knew what a precious moment it was as they kept watching the riders and horses.

Felicia said, "Wee Angel, it seems I knew and I didn't know that Sir William was important! Also I can't remember the name Jesus called him."

"Felicia! I can't remember the name either!" Wee Angel added. "Sometimes, it's just meant to be that way!"

Felicia and Wee Angel talked about the riders and everything that had gone on!

They looked at everything. The pathway went upwards into the sanctuary. On it's sides were also some pinnacles! Not too high above the hills, but they were glowing in their beauty!

"Wee Angel," Felicia spoke, "These fields of flowers, we're looking at are...oh! So beautiful!" Some of the flowers were like a short type of sunflower.

They watched Jesus and the riders fly across some of them.

"Just know, they can fly extremely fast if they want too, Felicia!" Wee Angel said.

"Felicia, we are going to fly this time." continued Wee Angel.

"Really!" said Felicia.

"You'll enjoy it!" giggled Wee Angel.

After watching these mighty winged horses open their wings, they felt their wings may not lift them up, but up they went off of the grassed area. They flew across some of the fields of flowers.

They flew very low, only a few feet above the flowers.

"Oh the fragrance of the flowers when we fly like this!" Felicia said again, "I love it!"

The roses and lilies were among these.

Because of everything, their hearts were filled with love. They flew just a short ways and landed on a golden pathway between the fields. There were lavenders to one side and deep purple irises to the other side.

Both played and sang! They ran... and ran.....and ran along the golden walkway. Other saints passed, while they did this. Some had been at the same service.

Some groupings of birds flew by them. Glories filled the heavenly sky.

They looked back at the hills and the pinnacles that formed the special service area.

Again, they were in flight, both having so much joy as they flew upwards, to the left, and then to the right.

"Felicia, see me!" Wee Angel would roll, twist as she flew, and circled Felicia.

Again, not far above the yellow flowers, then they would just hover and pick a flower."

"Isn't it nice to fly, Felicia?" said Wee Angel.

Felicia answered, "It's awesome! I never knew flying could be so wonderful!"

They saw some other angels flying, so they flew by them, waved, said hi's, smiled, laughed, and giggled!

Pretty soon, the larger angels and them flew in circles, up and down, enjoying the heavenly love!

They said their good days and they were away again!

They flew over streams, more fields, and onward!

Soon they came to a grouping of very tall, pine trees.

In the distance were some mountains, low mountains, but very beautiful!

They had passed this before in flight on Sir William. Pretty soon Wee Angel saw someone special!

"Look!" said Wee Angel, "Look! Look who's walking there, Tuddley Teddy!"

"Oh! Tuddley! Expressed Felicia.

So over they flew to him. He was busy walking through these trees. To the sides of the pines were other trees such as maple, weeping willows, and many fruit trees such as cherry trees.

Both landed and gave him the biggest hug. He bubbled with excitement.

"Thank you, Wee Angel for bringing me to see him again!" Felicia said.

They rode around on his back, walked through trees, played, sang songs of love.

Wee Angel said to Felicia, "We are going to keep flying! We came here just to say a quick 'Hi' to Tuddley Teddy. They said their good days, and gave hugs.

"I'll see you again, Tuddley!" said Felicia.

"Me too!" spoke up Wee Angel.

Felicia flew by a rose bush, picked a rose, then flew and placed it in Tuddley's fur up by his ears.

"There, " she said, "that's for you!"

Off they flew above the trees, around and through them as they were more in a wooded area. There was a stream which flowed through these very straight trees. The fragrance of these pines was awesome!

The branches with the needles were fairly high up on the trunks! Everything is alive in heaven. No dead branches!

"Remember, Felicia, we are in woods! You've got to fly a little differently here." said Wee Angel.

An angel came flying closer to them. In fact, then there were several angels and the one said to Wee Angel, "After you show Felicia a few places, you are to take her to the Lord's city."

Wee Angel listened and both made ready for the trip.

As they were flying, they parted with the angel, who flew on his way.

Wee Angel and Felicia talked, and then started onward, and then headed toward the Lord's city.

Chapter 5

Onward Looking at Heaven

Both Felicia and Wee Angel flew together over streams, fields of flowers, groupings of trees. There were animals with deer, and even buffalo. Birds were close at hand!

"Wee Angel, as I've said so many times! Heaven is so special! Thank you, Wee Angel for all you are doing and your friendship." Felicia talked as they flew over some patch type fields of flowers, including lilies, tulips, orchids, and more irises.

Of course, both flew, played, sang, flew in circles, flew up and lower again, landed often, many times by trees, many times flew around trees and also through the trees.

Right now, both decided to land by a grove of apple trees, some with blossoms, some with apples, nice big apples!

They wanted to eat! And eat they did!

"I'm going to show you another special place. It's very pretty!" spoke Wee Angel with a big apple in her hand.

Both sat under a tree, ate, talked, smiled, and looked at everything around them.

"See over by the edge of the trees, there's another golden walkway! We'll follow it!" said Wee Angel.

They still saw parts of the sanctuary with its pinnacles on some of it's sides amongst the hilly area that made up the sanctuary.

They saw the mighty glories above, stretched out over the heavenly land.

These glories went high upward into the heavenly sky! Remember part of these glories were where the angels were hovering, standing in heavenly glory as they sang in the mighty worship service. These glories about the hillside and above are always there. It's like a wall of light with power, but all peaceful, joyful, and awesome to look at them.

"It's so beautiful, Wee Angel!" again Felicia smiled, yet almost with tears as she looked at these glories.

Wee Angel said, "Felicia, there are levels to the glories. I don't know what that means, but as one goes upward in them, you just know it and feel it. The glories are so strong that the angels do not even use their wings as the glories strength holds them up! Remember everything floats to the heavenly lands, somewhat softly to the eyes.

As they sat there, they noticed others on the golden pathway; also angels flew above and over the fields.

When finished, they were on the golden way through more forested trees, bushes, and shrubs.

"Felicia, now we are going to a special place! These are special waterfalls, special in a very beautiful way! Just know that! I was going to wait to show you, but I'm too excited and we are very close to them." explained Wee Angel. "Wee Angel, can we just take time and pray again! Softly spoke Felicia.

"We are going to pray." Wee Angel said, "Wait just a short time. We are just about there."

They continued to walk on this glorious golden, sand-like, pebble-like, even feathery, heavenly path.

Soon they came to an open area in the trees. The trees were of many varieties with beautiful greens, burgundies, purples, and lavenders.

It had beautiful lilac bushes all around it's edges, again with plush grass.

There were benches, again of different types of woods, and small flowers over the edges of the woods. These were cushioned with a special fabric. Very soft, and the fabric had a glow to it. Very soft, very pretty! There were others of heaven and in prayer.

Both sat down on a bench.

There was short grass and even small flowers that grew, even if walked on all the time.

"We, just thank you, Jesus! We thank you for what you do and who you are! I love you." softly spoke Wee Angel.!"

"And me too!" softly added Felicia.

Then at the same time, "We love you!" said Felicia and Wee Angel.

They listened to the others in prayer.

They noticed several angels, hovering above the area, again singing in a heavenly language, glories to the Father.

As they left, they talked to several. There was June, Sharron, Rodney and Jason.

They shared, even gave hugs. Felicia and Wee Angel walked on, laughed, giggled, sometimes even shouted, talked loud, and praised the Lord.

They picked flowers, threw pebbles, flew around a tree or two, then sat on a bench or two. On they walked, on the golden way, in this the joy of heaven.

Daniel Leske

Chapter 6

A Waterfall of Light

As they walked along, Wee Angel said, "You know this place is different in a very heavenly way."

"I'm having so many blessings, love and joy, Wee Angel. It's been so awesome!" answered Felicia.

"This is heaven, Felicia! You know that!"

They were still in an area of trees. Big, tall, straight up and all were very alive! They walked upwards into hills as their pathway went more and more up hill, with trees on the slopes.

Soon they could see higher, and the area got more filled with glories.

The light got much stronger to their heavenly eyes, yet they felt so great!

"See Felicia, in the open area ahead is the waterfall." excited Wee Angel spoke to her.

"Oh look at that!" added Felicia. "It's the waters falling. Look at it's sides and around it. It looks like light falling."

"We can only go so close. Don't worry, Felicia, we are safe. We are in heaven!"

There were rocks to their sides, and more beautiful flowers amongst them. Mountain type flowers and little flowers, and they were very plush.

Felicia flew over to a couple, picked them and flew to Wee Angel and said, "Here you are, Wee Angel. See, I flew, picked them and flew them to you. I'm much better at flying and it's so much fun!"

"You are doing so good at it. Thank you, Felicia for the flowers." answered Wee Angel as she smelled their beautiful fragrance.

"These are little purple flowers. They maybe are little, but their fragrance is awesome." Wee Angel answered.

"Wee Angel, how beautiful and pretty these flowers smell!" said Felicia.

"Felicia, they are not the same as on earth. They are special flowers that go with all this light and glories." explained Wee Angel. "God makes them that way!"

There were other colors too!

There were some very special bushes about the steeper hillsides.

These bushes had a clear look to them. Some had on the petals, and on the edges of colored flowers was a reflection of rainbow colors from all the glories about the falls.

Again, just in this area, were special bushes with flowers. Some like our lilacs.

All the trees, rocks, everything took on a very lighted look, just like they were totally aglow!

They walked past the trees and reached the very open area. The falls was still quite a distance from them, but it was as far as they could go! They just knew they were not to go further.

"Wee Angel, there's no mountains or hills above the falls." as Felicia jumped up and down with excitement.

She went on, "Where's the water coming from?"

The waters went downward, to where they were at the lower level. The sides of the mountain or steep hill went upwards from them, and then looked like it molded into the light or glories of light.

But the water came from further up and up and up, they could not see the top.

All around the sides and above were these glories streaming downward!

It was a falls like one sees in the mountains, but no top to it.

"Felicia, it's coming through a doorway inside of tremendous light." explained Wee Angel.

"I don't understand it, just is!" continued Wee Angel.

Felicia said, "It looks like rainbows going up and down to the sides of the water."

Tremendous rainbows of light, yet it had the brightness of light itself, because it was light. There some clouds above as well in it's beauty. It seemed to mold into everything about it.

The waters in heaven came down so gently, very slowly, and so majestic. The falls again was not real wide, just mountain wide, as we have on earth.

Even the open area was aglow with light.

"Felicia, remember the Lord wants you to see special places in heaven. They are here! Many of them!" Wee Angel continued. "I ask God so many questions as you know! He said that the special places like this, his city, mountain, and others around heaven, help to keep the heavenly lands all lite, nice even light. So there's no darkening of things."

"Oh! Wee Angel, that's great! Isn't that awesome?" said Felicia.

Other saints of heaven were coming there.

Felicia prayed, "Thank you God for your glories and this beautiful waterfall."

Both walked back down the golden pathway as there was only one way there.

They sat on rocks, flew around rocks, listened to the beautiful birds, and looked at little ones like squirrels, chipmunks, raccoons, and other animals of heaven.

Chapter 7

Annie

As they walked down the mountain hillside, enjoying everything, Wee Angel said "Look! Look! Over there, Felicia!"

"A big cat!" Exclaimed Felicia.

"Yes! It's Annie! Oh! You'll love, Annie."

She saw Wee Angel and headed towards them.

Annie was a cougar. She had the most beautiful coat. She had some rings of fur around her neck. They were a little darker than her coat color. Three rings made with a little brown, then white, a little brown, then white, a little brown.

Wee Angel flew towards her and flew around through the trees along the mountain hillside.

Felicia waited on the golden pathway, watched and thanked the Lord as she watched Wee Angel in flight.

She said, "Thank you God for Wee Angel who watched me on earth, and, now she is showing me around heaven, and in meeting you too! I love you!"

She raised her arms and praised God and then shouted through the trees, "Just know I love you, Lord!"

Shortly after Wee Angel and Annie were there, then began the hugs.

"Oh! She is so wonderful!" smiled Felicia as she had her arms around Annie's neck, holding her as tight as she could!

Felicia said, "I want her to come with us."

"She will!" answered Wee Angel.

Annie jumped and danced about on her legs.

Then Felicia noticed, "Look, Wee Angel, she has wings on her sides."

"Of course," answered Wee Angel, "there are some animals in heaven that have them. The large horse flies a lot, but other animals that would or could fly, don't fly as much! So you don't always see them

in the heavenly skies. It seems that way, but they do have wings if needed!" Wee Angel continued, "The Lord keeps the heavenly sky for angels, those from earth that received wings, horses with wings,

and his birds. Annie is blessed with wings."

After heaven's time, they walked on to a place where another golden path branched off their path. They followed it, Wee Angel, Felicia, and Annie.

Annie ran about them, and just felt wonderful about her two little friends!

They were on the low side of the hills, still in trees, that were along the stream from the waterfall.

The trees lessened and then Wee Angel spoke, "See ahead Felicia!"

There along the pathway was about a dozen cherry trees with big beautiful cherries!"

"Wow! It couldn't be better!" said Felicia as they ran towards them.

Both ate, climbed trees, and sat on the limbs.

During this Annie ran around the trees.

Many birds were in the area. Little rabbits ran about, which were different colored and different sizes.

Felicia wanted to wade out into the waters of the large stream from the falls. Both played in the stream, sang, and splashed water. Annie laid on the bank near them.

As they played they noticed an angel flying towards them.

The angel landed and said to Wee Angel, "Why don't you take Felicia to the archway in the mountains. Then after that head to the Lord's city.

It was time for resting..... and resting..... and resting!

As all did so, by the cherry trees and beautiful stream, on the low side of the mountain hillside. The grass was nice and plush, as always with flowered bushes about them.

Along the stream were beautiful hedges. They had little flowers on them in colors like pinks, yellows, even golden flowers. The scene was awesome.

They saw above, heavenly glories from the falls.

Several birds landed by them and walked up to them, couple of sparrows, even a egret. A couple of other birds that liked to be in streams, walked up to them too!

"Aren't they nice, Wee Angel." as Felicia touched the birds and talked to them.

Wee Angel answered, "Remember they'll come to you when you want! Then they will slowly fly or walk away from you."

She went on, "The animals are the same way as they will come out of the forests, meadows, grazing lands, and walk to the saints of heaven. Then walk with them along the golden ways or wherever they go to, although they have to wait outside the special areas or even the Lord's city.

So often as Wee Angel and Felicia traveled, they saw animals with saints. They were enjoying his little ones.

Chapter 8

At the Archway

After much rest, they were ready to go to the archway. Annie included!

Felicia and Wee Angel wanted Annie with them, so with them she went!

Up they flew, above the stream.

Wee Angel called to Felicia, "We'll fly along the stream. It goes along the base of this mountain range to where we want to go!"

Again the mountains were not real high, but bigger than hills. They flew along, and at times they flew very fast!

Quickly, they flew, Felicia was stunned by the speed, but she was at peace with it. It was a part of her gift as she came to heaven.

They followed the stream, which would curve left and right about the base of the mountains.

They winged past groupings of trees, flowerbeds, orchards, special groupings of bushes, and lake-like areas with the golden paths about to everywhere! There saw many saints.

The mountains they flew along were for the most part with trees, pine-like trees in areas(like our pines on earth but heavenly different). As on earth some of the pines in some areas were a richer, deeper green. These were a deeper green.

Remember, in heaven, there are no shadows as the light is so evenly balanced.

Finally their flying slowed, including Annie who flew right with them the whole heavenly time.

"Look at the archway in the mountains." Felicia said, as they flew closer and it still was a ways ahead of them.

The mountainsides were very golden, rose straight up, and the archway was in between this. Flowers were up and down the mountainsides, golden hues surrounded the archway, again a lot of glories, and light surrounded this archway.

Felicia looked up, "Look at the glories above this range! Look at them!"

"It's special, Felicia." as Wee Angel looked. "As all places are in different ways."

They flew ahead praising God, and praises came to their lips and praises flowed from their little mouths. Even Annie had a special sound coming from her mouth as they neared this archway or entrance. There were glories of light all around it!

Then they landed on the golden walkway.

Soon an angel came flying towards them. She landed near them and greeted them.

Wee Angel knew her.

"How are you doing, Wee Angel? My name is Angel Heather. I'll be going with you."

"My name is Felicia." as both gave heavenly hugs.

Wee Angel and Angel Heather talked and talked! Annie enjoyed the moment.

Soon they were walking onward!

All they could really see were a lot of glories which filled everything, including the gate, yet the mountains were there.

"Felicia, just know that once through this gate, we'll start flying upward." as Wee Angel told Felicia what to do in this light.

Wee Angel went on, "We are going to one of the Lord's mansions as he calls them. Now the distance from here can be close or they can be extremely great. This is heaven, Felicia, and heaven is vast!"

Angel Heather added, "This is why I am going with you. It's what I do!"

She went on, "At this archway gate one has to have wings to go where we are going. So everyone can't go there! We are guided all the way, once we start on this journey."

Wee Angel said, "We'll take Annie with us. She can go there as long as she is with us."

Then they walked through the gate, light all around yet the sides to the mountains were steep and canyon-like! There was even another stream, by the archway that flowed to another stream that followed the mountains.

Wee Angel continued, "Now we will be flying upwards, very quickly in this light and power. It will guide us as we fly upwards in the light!"

So in the light,..........in the light,............ in the light,.......... and on, they flew!

On and on they flew in the light!

As they flew, all they could see was just more light. Light was all around them.

There was so much peace! They knew they were all right!

Then ahead in the light, they saw another heavenly entrance, golden all around, feathery-like gates or hedges. Inside the clouds, tall hedges of trees went away from the gate, which had some flowers too!

As they flew near, neither spoke much during this, the Lord's power just guided them. Through this gate, they flew! Then it was golden and trees were very golden, and tall!

The floor of the forest was golden, and yet the most beautiful greens were on the leaves. The waters flowing had another golden hue, but waters as water should be!

They noticed everything seemed, even more of light and more celestial. Everything was even brighter then where they came from in heaven.

This has to do with the glories of light and the power of it!

They could see in the distance, yet it was a special place, like a mansion of forest land with trees, surrounded by glories, above the mountain lands, heavenly lands!

The heavenly land here was more glass-like or the likeness of crystal in appearance. In some ways, some of the light went right through everything like a window glass. Everything appeared more glowing!

They landed there.

Felicia said, "Everything is glowing in light!"

"It's a mansion of heaven and it's a part of heaven!" answered Wee Angel.

Angel Heather, "I'll be with you the whole journey, and we'll go back to where we started from at the mountains."

Many angels were gathered there! They saw small groupings of them. The had instruments and sang praises to God.

Many angels were about!

"Is this their home?" asked Felicia.

"In some ways, it is Felicia!" added Wee Angel. "As I said, only those with wings can come here."

It was so like an outdoor home and the angels went about talking, singing, and praising God. Also they flew in and out through the gateway.

"The Lord said mansions." added Wee Angel. "That can mean a lot, just know they are beautiful! There are so many different places as mansions! All very beautiful in their own way!"

"It's awesome here!" added Felicia.

There were orchids, climbing roses, dahlias, special flowers, special trees, places to sit and talk, walk and fly, also special fruits not known on earth.

There were special glowing lights of glory all over and much more!

"Just beautiful!" Felicia said.

Wee Angel flew towards some tree trunks and called, "Look Felicia! Keep watching me!"

She flew around a couple of trunks, "See!"

Felicia said, "I can see you right through the tree trunk as you flew around it."

Wee Angel flew back and said, "It is that way here. Now where we flew from in heaven you could see through as well, but this is even more so!"

Wee Angel went on, "In heaven and these mansion the light is so much a part of everything and how it can pass through that there again are no shadows. Everywhere the light is so even as well! Except the glories and God's city!"

Wee Angel went on, "It's something like that!"

Felicia said, "I always think of the golden path and how we can see so deep into it and it seems to radiate light. The leaves, flowers, and how they look like they are glowing, because the light is passing through and also we can see through a lot of them!"

"As you said, Wee Angel, here it's even more so! Felicia continued. "It's so beautiful! Everywhere we have gone!"

Annie, of course, was being hugged by angels and more angels as they approached her.

She loved it! They loved it!

So many angels, a beautiful mansion above heavenly lands. The joy of heaven is so real.

Daniel Leske

Chapter 9

A Beautiful Place

The three were awed by all about them! There were pearl-like gems and tables there with special gems and having gems of many different colors. These were apart of small walls and waterfalls, and out of door type areas where the angels were standing or sitting!

Many talked with Angel Heather, Felicia and Wee Angel. And as often, Wee Angel always was the smallest of the angels. If they were about her size, they still were a little bigger than her. It seemed the other angels knew this.

Annie was being well taken care of as well!

There were also different levels here with stairways and patio type areas, again decorated in gems to make up the walls to these areas as one walked up to them.

These were all open! It was a main open area where Felicia, Wee Angel, and Annie stood and looked at everything.

There were special, glowing, small arbors about them, to both sides of Annie, Felicia and Wee Angel.

The area seemed so holy to them.

Felicia had to ask "Wee Angel, Look! How far does it go?"

"It's hard to explain, Felicia, but it's like a very huge outdoor room. Some, you can only go so far, others you can go on and on! And it goes upward with steps and stairways, many levels. And, as you know, angels can fly, but they can walk too! It's made for both."

"It is like a home!" added Felicia, "An angel home!"

Felicia went on, "Angel Heather, your hair is always sparkling with light. It looks so beautiful!"

Angel Heather had golden hair with browns. She said, "Thank you, Felicia for the compliment. My hair is that way because I'm in the light stream so much!"

Both noticed how she sparkled all over, beaming with light.

They walked along the special, stoned pathway with gems onward to another area. There were a lot of trees, beautiful lighted trees with acorns like glowing gems on them. These were aglow all the time!

There were many gems like a pillar and to the outside, flowers, and climbing flowers! Small streams of water flowed about, along the pathways, and also pools of water were there too!

They walked through the archway into glorious light and soon flew again upwards, fast and quick!

Seemingly without effort, they traveled this way going steeply upwards and then through another archway. This was higher, and it was walled by gems, another heavenly home.

It was similar to the other one, again angels and also some saints with wings were there too!

They visited and gave out hugs.

"This is so beautiful, Wee Angel," Felicia said, "and different from what we've done! The holiness of angels about them."

"I know, Felicia!" added Wee Angel. "All I know, I'm to show you different places in heaven! You'll be back here."

"But there is so much!" answered Felicia.

They walked on and up some of the stairways and to open areas.

Then Angel Heather was met by another special angel who asked them to follow her. Her name was Angel Michelle.

She took them to this special room. As they entered this room, they could see the heavens past heaven.

They could see the universe like we do at night!

"Look at the stars." said Felicia.

As they looked to the sides and outward, they saw tremendous glories of light streaming outward from where they were looking in this room. These streams of light did not interfere with what they seeing about the heavens.

The room was not too small, with total openness to the heavens.

Felicia saw very large, streams of light going out and away to the sides of the open view.

"Felicia," Wee Angel said. "Just know that is for a reason of travel."

Wee Angel didn't say any more on it.

Felicia knew and felt it had to do with the angels traveling to other places(mansions) and even earth.

Felicia sensed earth out there, but she couldn't see earth as she talked to Wee Angel.

"Just know it's there, Felicia." finished Wee Angel.

They talked with Angel Michelle. She was explaining much to them, as well as giving Annie a big hug.

She said, "Look up again."

They saw all light, many colors of light. Then it was like a curtain opened and they saw planets close up, then with distance or fairly close a star from the heavens. Then they saw this planet called earth.

They saw a sea around it and it troubled Wee Angel and Felicia.

Angel Heather said, "It has to do with the times, and the season. You have a reason for being troubled about it. It's not for us to talk about, Felicia."

Then there was a bright light that went over everything they looked at! Then the heavens were back as they had looked before!

As Felicia looked at the heavens, she said, "I remember Daniel telling me the most beautiful moment in his life about our Creator. Daniel said one night he looked into the heavens. Then he said, he saw the face of God amongst the stars in the deep heavens. His face covered so much of the outer space amongst the stars. God had the whitest hair he ever had seen! His beard was snow white, and his eyes were like wisdom and eternity. They were so piercing! Then after 10 to 20 seconds his face pulled back into the heavens. He said God's face is so handsome. Daniel did a picture of this. After that Daniel understood what David said about God and seeking his face. Daniel always felt that David had seen the Creator's face in the heavens many times. As I said Daniel said it was the most powerful 10 to 20 seconds on his whole being."

"Thank you, Felicia for sharing that!" both Angel Michelle and Angel Heather said together.

All of them formed a circle and prayed together.

Felicia prayed, "Thank you Lord God our Creator, for being you and your creation. Thank you that we can be some a small part of it, and we pray for earth, everyone on it that they would know you and come to know you, and come to know you through the Way you want them to, through your son, Jesus. Amen!"

With this moment there were tears, for they knew how special the Creator is for us all.

Then there were some hugs as they prepared to go on another journey. Angel Michelle said, "Please come and see me again. It's been so nice with you and Annie."

Wee Angel and Felicia promised they would see her.

Angel Michelle showed them another archway.

She said, "This will take you back to the first archway."

After they left this room, with Angel Heather leading, they flew straight ahead, yet they sensed they were heading lower in direction. They flew on....... and on....... and on....... an on!

Soon they came to an archway of light and the sides of the mountain, but along the same stream.

"My! Oh my! Now I'm starting to understand heaven more!" said Felicia.

Wee Angel nodded, "This is heaven!"

"I hope you enjoyed the journey and I hope I can see you again, too!" as Angel Heather gave them hugs, including Annie.

They praised the Lord and thanked the Lord for being there! Annie was happy too!

Each said to Annie how nice she traveled with them.

Chapter 10

April and Hope

All three walked along this stream, about the base of the mountains. "Wee Angel, can I ask you what the stream is called?" asked Felicia.

"Why, yes!" answered Wee Angel with a fresh picked flower in her hand. It's called the Glorious Stream."

Felicia added, "There's a golden light coming from these waters."

Wee Angel agreed.

"Felicia," she said, "these streams are totally pure. The plant life is always alive. It just is!"

Wee Angel went on, "The fragrances are always pleasing and sometimes very fragrant. There is a difference from earth. No death here! On earth there is death, at all levels, both man, animals, and vegetation. As I've said, our eyes are different here because there is so much more light. Our bodies are celestial as well! It has to do with the light!"

They stood and surveyed the horizons of open fields of flowers with the mountains to the sides. Some hills, many flocks of birds, some ducks, the stream birds, egrets......... and more!

They saw many glories above these mountains.

They saw the glories of God's city in the heavenly skies. Many golden light glories, light aqua greens in color for radiance.

Annie, of course, was right with them.

She often ran around them and seemingly was excited about everything. She loved to walk with Wee Angel on one side and Felicia on the other side. She liked their hugs too!

They were a sight to see as Felicia and Wee Angel weren't that tall! Annie was a tall cougar. She was just so happy to be with them, as Annie would always be looking at Felicia and Wee Angel for guidance. Annie wanted to do everything she could to be close to them!

"I'm just in awe of heaven." Felicia said as they walked along with Annie in between them.

"Felicia, you were only in two of these special mansions." added Wee Angel.

They noticed a couple of fruit trees ahead of them along the path and the Glories Stream.

The three took off and flew to it.

These were some peach trees. About the base of them were some patches of strawberries, close by a few raspberries. No thorns!

All three ate, including Annie. She liked fruits too!

As they sat, several saints walked past them on the walkway. They had their greeting and walked on!

They noticed several angels flying by the base of the mountains. Then some saints on the backs of winged horses, came flying past them.

"That's so beautiful, Wee Angel!" as Felicia continued, "I can't get enough of seeing these flying horses, some by themselves, some with riders, and some even are with angel riders. It does something to me."

She went on, "We didn't have that on earth, and yet horses on earth were so beautiful! I know by the Bible that God loves them so much! Now I understand!"

Wee Angel prayed, "Lord, thank you for your horses and your winged horses. Yes thank you, Lord God for your creation. Don't ever stop creating, because we love to see it! Your places and mansions, that you build for us."

"Thank you! We love you." added Felicia.

Both had some tears in their eyes. Annie was now humble too, as she knew in her heart that this is special.

Wee Angel said, "When God walks his lands whether in heaven or on earth, everything created knows him as he goes by them."

Felicia remembered a song that the Holy Spirit had given Daniel and her on earth."

Wee Angel said, "I know it too! It was so pretty!"

Felicia said, "The song was called 'In the Morning! In the Morning!'"

She went on:

"In the morning, in the morning"

"God walks our land."

"In the morning, in the morning"

"He holds your hand."

"All creatures great"

"All creatures small."

"In the morning, in the morning"

"Answer God's call."

Felicia went on humming it, then said "That's all I remember of it. There's more verses."

"I remember Daniel, humming that!" answered Wee Angel.

Then out from the mountainside over and between some trees flew two parrots.

Wee Angel called to them, "April and Hope! Come here! I want you to meet Felicia."

Wee Angel knew that Annie knew them. Both flew towards them and came, landed on a branch of the fruit tree. Wee Angel told Felicia all about them. Felicia was already touching their heads and talking to them. The parrots spoke beautiful sounds.

"They will be with us for awhile!" said Wee Angel, "Felicia, isn't it nice to have friends. Let's talk awhile, eat awhile, and then we are going to another special place in heaven."

Chapter II

A Beautiful Prayer Area

"Felicia, we are going to another prayer place." said Wee Angel.

"It's very beautiful." finished Wee Angel.

So up they flew using their wings, continued along the stream at the base of the mountains.

Wee Angel, Felicia, Annie, April, and Hope, all of them together!

They flew just above the glorious golden way. Sometimes over and above the Glories Stream too!

On and on and on they flew, pretty fast at times!

Then in heaven's time they landed back on a golden way.

The stream curved from the mountain and across the land of heaven. Also they walked, up small hills and upward more!

April and Hope loved the ride they got on Annie's back.

Pretty soon along the sides were rows and rows of grape vines filled with grapes. They were different colors, very large, and juicy!

They enjoyed some grapes!

Then on they walked, and then amidst the grapes on the heaven's grass was a smaller buffalo.

He was white and grayish in color, larger than a buffalo calf, yet he pretty well looked like a full grown buffalo, with a beard. Wee Angel called to him and he ran and stood by them with the two parrots on the back of Annie.

"Oh he's beautiful!" said Felicia, "He's a lot like Tuddley."

"What's his name?" Felicia asked.

"It's Longstreet, Felicia." said Wee Angel.

"Longstreet the buffalo! I like that.!

"Do you want Longstreet to come with us for awhile!" said Wee Angel.

"Absolutely!" answered Felicia.

Longstreet loved hugs, he was happy, could be hugged like Tuddley and he smiled ear to ear.

They headed upwards slowly away from the main mountains and more into the hills as they were still along side the mountains. They still passed grapes that were along the sides of the golden path.

Then along this golden path on both sides were white blossomed apple trees which lined the way for quite some distance. There were more fruit trees on both sides. All with fruit: apples, cherries mainly, and some others.

Then ahead on the hill, it leveled flat on top!

They saw another prayer area ahead of them! Then further ahead on the sides of another golden way was an archway. Bushes of climbing roses, clementis flowers were on both sides of the entrance. To the sides of this hill were all olive trees filled with olives.

Annie and Longstreet stayed on the lands outside the prayer area. The animals just knew that! The two parrots flew to some fruit trees, Annie walked, and laid under one of the apple trees.

Inside was a very large open area with saints. Hedges were to the sides, and above these one saw the trees.

There was an opening in the hedge to the trees. All around was a row of cherry trees with a path through this, then another hedge around the very outside. Then outside further were rows and rows of olive trees that were loaded with olives.

The saints were in prayer, some stood, some walked, some knelt, some were laying on these special holy grounds, others sat on special God made seats, and others with arms uplifted praising God.

Some went and others came through the trees, and were on the hillsides.

Outside the level area of the hills and the slopes were gentle rolling hills with these trees.

"Look above!" Wee Angel said.

They could barely see the higher mountains because of the glories of light.

"More angels!" said Felicia.

They hovered above, sang glories, praised with beautiful heavenly sounds, harmonies, some solo's, some played instruments, and soft for prayer.

As they stood in heaven's time, some angels had brass instruments and played a mighty sound of praise,

They put the horns aside as others praised the Lord and then more songs went forth.

Felicia said, "Wee Angel, it looks like some of them are standing in the glories."

Both prayed and prayed and prayed!

They walked amongst the trees and fruit trees. They prayed some more!

With all that had happened for the two, it was time to spend more time in prayer and pray, they did!

Praise, they did!

Sing songs, they did!

Listening to the angels, and looking at the angels, they did!

This was a very holy, holy place in heaven.

The angels here were special, yet all in heaven were special too, for whatever they did, was to please the Creator!

Their living was so filled with love – love – love, and more love! Love that grows mightily within, over filling their being! Their belonging!

Quietly, they walked, with others that came and went as well!

They stayed as long as they wanted too!

Soon they walked outside this special area. Back with their friends, with greetings between each, and ready to go again, filled with this joy. This joy of being in heaven.

Chapter 12

Walking Along Heaven's Land

They walked back on the same way, away from the prayer grounds. Both parrots, one was on Annie and one on Longstreet.

The songs still flowed from the lips of Wee Angel and Felicia. After a short time, there was another golden way, which headed out and away from the mountains. They were still in some small hills, as they headed more towards open heavenly lands.

After heaven's time, they were in fields of flowers. Some groupings of angels flew above them. They passed other saints, and to their one side was a field of lilies.

"Remember, Felicia," said Wee Angel, " I first saw you in the field of lilies."

"I remember so well, Wee Angel, I remember! Thank you, again!"

These lilies were white. Then on the other side, there were lavender, flowers like the tulips on earth. Then as they walked on there were purple and white flowers, like zinnias, violets, asters and others. Pretty soon flowers everywhere! Tulips and more tulips were some of them.

There were some streams that went about, through the flowers, and their golden paths would cross them.

A grouping of evergreens was there too! On they walked, they had too, because Longstreet had no wings. Inside Wee Angel seemed to know that for

Felicia to meet the little ones, walking on the golden path was a good way. But fun they had, Annie, Longstreet and the two parrots.

April and Hope were now on Wee Angel's and Felicia's shoulders. They walked and had a nice time playing with the two birds and the animals. There was little grass areas along the golden paths. Longstreet and Annie would run about with Felicia, Wee Angel, April, and Hope flying circles about them.

Wee Angel spoke out, "Thank you Lord, for our friends."

In time, they got further from the hills and closer to more trees. Soon they came to more bushes and also hedges that went out and away from the golden way.

The hedges went around some groves of palm trees. The vegetation was much the same. There were hedges around these groves of palm trees which often were squared like many of the fields of flowers.

There were golden paths that went to these beautiful groves with plush vegetation and flowers. There were streams of water with small waterfalls that flowed along side of the hedges with flowers. It was beautiful to see how the hedges surrounded these areas with tropical trees amidst the fields of flowers.

In heaven, the trees don't have to be in special climates like on earth. They enjoyed everything about them. Felicia and Wee Angel knew they wanted to fly to the Lord's city. Everyone knew and so all their good days were said, as well as hugs. Annie had such a good time with Longstreet and the two parrots. Both Felicia and Wee Angel took their turns sitting on Longstreet.

Felicia said, "Next time I'm going to spend more time riding on him."

They took some time to spend with them before they would go on towards God's city.

Both said, "We'll see you again!"

Wee Angel said, "In heaven, it just happens that way, that we will see them again!"

Then Longstreet the white buffalo, April, and Hope, the parrots went on their way. April and Hope flew towards the palm trees while Longstreet walked along the golden path towards an area with open grass.

Wee Angel said, "Longstreet will graze and rest, and then he'll go with more saints or angels. They love his company."

Annie stayed with Wee Angel and Felicia.

Wee Angel would always say, "Felicia, we'll see them again! Annie, you'll see them too! This is heaven."

Chapter 13

Back to the Lord's City

Up in the heavenly sky, Wee Angel, Felicia, and Annie flew!

They flew just above the flowered lands, and just above the trees.

Onward they flew with Wee Angel leading them.

After a heavenly time, they saw more glories forming mightily above the heaven's land from God's city.

They flew by some special little falls with some bushes. Wee Angel said, "Felicia, let's take a little time and rest!"

So they flew and landed on the soft grass by some bushes that had beautiful orange flowers on them. Nearby were some swans in the pools of water by a small stream with small waterfalls. Also a couple of streams flowed through this area. There were very colorful birds that liked streams and shallow waters.

Even Annie found a berry bush to eat it's berries.

Wee Angel spotted a tree that was similar to the banana tree. The fruit was smaller, but just as delicious. Wee Angel flew to it and brought some back for Felicia. There they rested and again enjoyed talking, along with the eating of food.

There in the distance, not too far, were hills with a lot of trees. Many of the areas of trees were like the fields of flowers in that there was one kind to the hill or area.

Wee Angel knew that it was time to part with Annie. This took some doing!

"I hoped she could be with us, yet!" said Felicia.

Wee Angel said, "We're going to the Lord's city. She'd have to wait outside anyway, so we'll let Annie go here."

Annie just seemed to know this.

They gave many hugs. Annie had been so much fun for them.

"We'll see you again!" said Wee Angel and Felicia.

The three flew again, separated, and Annie flew towards the forested hillsides. Their hearts were filled with joy! It was from the great times they were having in heaven.

Onward Felicia and Wee Angel flew towards the glories of the city.

They flew, and neared the city from this direction. This was different from the other times.

The land was getting hillier and they could see the mighty mountain of God, rising high into the heavenly sky. They could not see the top, as it rose upwards into the light and glories.

The city was around the base of the mighty holy mountain. It was not a small city, but very large and very long in any direction.

Very spacious whether in heaven, or if it was on earth."

Many names for it, but Wee Angel said, "I just like to say it is God's city or The Lord's city. It is his. It is his Mighty Holy City! It is his land and holy dwelling place.

The glories rose upward from the whole city, but stronger as one looked upwards to the heavenly skies. They flew closer and closer, then saw it from a distance.

DANIEL

They flew above the trees and many of them. So as they had gotten closer, there were trees on both sides of this golden walkway. Here they landed so they could walk or fly into the city. The trees were beautiful trees like the sequoia on earth. They were very open on the bottom sides with grass, and rose bushes. Streams of water flowed everywhere through these trees. Here, were hills by the city. The streams flowed so softly.

They walked on, still in the trees on the golden way when they came to the edge of the trees. Then a river-like stream flowed under the golden way. On the left side were waterfalls from a level above, and on the right side another falls, which went to a lower level. Felicia and Wee Angel were on the topside. The trees went up to this river and then ended on the side near the gate. By this gate on the other side of the river were high pinnacles, which went along the river. These pinnacles rose high above, very mountain-like pinnacles. They were needle shaped formations. Some were short in length, and others were long and slender.

Felicia said, "How beautiful they are!"

Out of them came tremendous light and colors, as we see in rainbows.

Felicia said, "I can't believe what I'm seeing! Oh my, Wee Angel!"

Both were so awed by it. Both stood in awe and reverence.

The gate also had pinnacles, and they were very high, yet there were small gems inside the pinnacles. So it looked gate-like in form, and lights from the pinnacle gems were soft and pleasing to their heavenly eyes.

All around the base and along the streams were flowers. Very thick with flowers and many climbing type flowers. On the trees side there were flower bushes, roses, hedges, some animals grazed about under the trees, saints walked, angels flew! Some winged horses as well waited for saints to go across the lands of heaven. It was a beautiful sight!

Chapter 14

The Beautiful Pinnacles

Wee Angel and Felicia looked at the streams with falls. The streams curved gently, out and away from the pinnacles. The streams were hidden by the trees as both looked at the horizon. The pinnacles along the stream seemed to mold gently into the mountainsides.

The pinnacles were very high! It was like a mountain canyon with one side trees. Again the trees were like the sequoias on earth. Then the falls and stream, with the other side, being high pinnacles that rose high above on the sides of the mountain.

The gate had small gems within the pinnacles.

As they entered the gate, the golds of the city streets were different than the heavenly lands.

Wee Angel said, "The mansions are still quite a distance ahead of us. We'll be going through these pinnacles and then we'll see the mansions of the city."

Special beyond special, no place on earth or heaven is like this city of God's, his own!

Wee Angel went on, "Now the mansion can be a special place and sometimes a very large place or area or it can be a dwelling place made with gems. Even an extremely vast patio open area as in God's city is like a mansion. One thing for sure, Felicia, these mansions are beautiful and we are only going to a couple of them. The Lord said he would make mansions. The mansions are awesome!"

As they walked, they still had pinnacles to both sides, but more like a valley, and as they walked, there were waterfalls, coming from fairly high above them. On both sides, the waters fell slowly into the streams that were a ways from them. All within the pinnacles with a look like gems or rocks as God had made them.

"Wee Angel, it looks like the waters come right out of the pinnacles above us!" Felicia said with excitement.

"It does! Doesn't it!" added Wee Angel.

Light beams from these pinnacles were everywhere as light went through them, and bounced off other pinnacles.

"It's like glories of bouncing lights!" said Wee Angel to Felicia.

She continued, "God's mountain is so that it is a part of light. Just like looking through crystal, and the pinnacles are parts of this. As we get to the mansions, you will see, how they seem to mold into God's mountain. It's because the light goes through the mountain and from the mountain. The Bible talks about the importance of the rock as a part of God and who he is! The diamonds are the hardest, and yet they are crystal clear. Keeping this in mind you can understand the awesomeness of God's mountain. It also shows the beauty of God in his creation.

As they walked, they greeted other saints, some angels.

They walked for quite awhile and enjoyed the pinnacles, the streams, more falls, then a real wide falls. Also there were many small falls, with pinnacles to the side. Also many awesome flowers, again roses and layered lavenders, and some beautiful yellow flowers.

"How beautiful, Wee Angel!" said Felicia.

In the distance ahead of them, they could see some mansions made from gems.

There were some very small gem mansions, then there were others large, and extremely large! Some were trimmed in gold, and some were trimmed in silver.

The stream was on both sides of the golden street as they walked, then a river flowed through the pinnacles on the left, and under the street to the right.

They stood and looked both ways.

By them, on both sides of this river were pinnacles, but in the distance there were like mansions that were right along the river. These rose upwards, because they were a part of the mountains or hills.

Glories of light were all over, very light, even on their heavenly eyes. They saw small streams of water coming into these other streams, rivers, and little many little falls.

They walked on the walkway amidst the mansions made by gems. Saints walked as well as angels.

"Look above!" said Wee Angel to Felicia.

They saw angels flying above as they walked along the golden street. The pinnacles of God's mountain were fewer, and the valley wider!

Ahead they saw these mansions located higher and higher to the sides and upward, as they walked closer to God's mountain that rose high above.......above........, and above!

Both flew along the golden street, with gem-like mansions, flowered waterfalls, streams, benches, saints, and angels!

So much to see as a city! It's very large, yet not overly done or crowded, yet very vast!

Wee Angel said, "The vastness to the Lord's city was around and out from the Lord's mountain, and the mansions in this city went upward around the mountain and yet away from the mountain."

Felicia said, "Look upwards, Wee Angel!"

"I see what you mean!" continued Felicia, "Look at the high walkways and balcony-like mansions. Some of these look like they are a part of the mountain and others molded right into the glories of light."

Wee Angel said, :"That's a wonderful way to describe them!"

They looked at some of the slopes of the mountainsides. They saw mansions seemingly molded into the mountainsides. As they walked in areas, away from the mountain, they looked up into the glories of the mountain. Through the light, they saw huge mansions that looked like they were floating in the light. There were platforms with walls made by gems, and gardens where saints could sit and visit! These would go up and away from the golden street.

First levels were molded into the mountainsides, or hillsides with rivers or streams about them.

Felicia and Wee Angel looked upward higher and higher, the levels were molded more into light itself.

It just was! That's how it looked to Felicia and Wee Angel. The mountainsides appeared like clear gems that light passed through, that gave this standing in the glories look to the mansions or garden areas. The stairways were in the glories of light, like they were in the heavenly sky above them.

Chapter 15

A Beautiful City

Wee Angel said Felicia, "You have to remember this is God's city and it is vast. We are in one part of it and there are so many beauties as you and I call them! There are rivers, streams, and the gold on the streets. The way God used the gems, how he created the falls, the mansions are different, all around this holy mountain. You and I are only seeing a small part of it."

"My! Wee Angel!" answered Felicia.

Wee Angel added, "It's so garden-like with what we see, yet a city with gems, mansions, yet vast and majestic!"

As they walked along the golden street, there were tremendous light and glories, above them! They walked in them."

Soon they were in an area of just gem-like mansions. These were very large, each mansion looked like one of God's gems in color and shaped with gold and silver trim.

They walked inside one mansion and there they saw saints and angels. There were angels on the sides who sang praises to God. There were small trees, bushes, gardens, and small waterfalls within the mansion. Everything was so alive!

"It's so alive!" Felicia said, "It's like outside, yet inside this mansion."

There were many areas in the mansion, patio's as we would call them, separate rooms, yet in the open, and on different levels with stairways. Some stairs were very short to another level or garden area, some with a lot of stairs to a higher level, yet most levels went from one to the next one. They were spaced so there was just a few steps to the next level and they were spaced very perfectly about this open area.

The garden-like levels had streams, of light going up and down it's edges, pleasing streams, very soft though to their heavenly eyes.

Wee Angel said to Felicia, "I'm going to show you something special soon!"

Angels flew to these, but there seemed to be orderliness to it, as they did so!

There were balconies and special railings of the finest woods. Everything was so balanced because of the gems, with waters, and with plant life. There were flowers, and small trees with the brightness of golden colors on the walkways.

There were levels and many of them, reached by these steps, one to the next! Yet, each so garden-like, and the balconies went out and away from the mansion. It's walls were clear, see through, and the color of the gem.

Some had red walls on it's sides, some blue, some purple, some green, the whole mansion with one color for the walls.

Some mansions were narrow, some very wide, others squared, and many different sizes.

They were along the streets, on mountainsides, with rivers, and waterfalls between them.

Both had left a mansion and again walked on the street of gold viewing everything around them. They both felt they should pray!

"Thank you again, Lord for your creation, your city, my friend Wee Angel. Thank you for showing so much! I love you!" prayed Felicia.

"We love to praise you, Lord for your creation, your city, and my friend, Wee Angel. Thank you for showing me so much! I love you!" prayed Felicia.

"We love to praise you, Lord!" prayed little Wee Angel.

Both were so awed and thankful for what they had seen, the saints, they had talked to and met there. Also they were thankful for the angels, that as they looked above, at different times, were there.

They saw groupings of the singing angels, which hovered above! They sang hallelujahs to their Father. Often this happened as they walked, and flew to different places in this city.

Some of the mansions were special prayer areas for the saints, and along the streets were areas where they could pray and praise the Lord. Everything was in harmony. Everything seemed to glorify the Father with life and living life for who He was and is!

It indeed was only a small part of his holy city, but it was His and Wee Angel knew it.

Again, tears of joy filled their eyes and little heavenly hearts as they saw all of this, and felt all of this, and enjoyed all of this!

Chapter 16

A Beautiful Waterfall and Sanctuary

As they left the huge mansion, along the golden street, Felicia said, "As we walk, everything seems so holy and alive. It seems everything is that way here."

"The colors of the different gold's that make up the streets, are so beautiful. They seem like the finest varieties of gold." finished Felicia.

Along the streets, at different times, were hedges with flowers on them, as there were sometimes streams of water by the street.

Soon they took another street, and they headed more towards the higher mountain, God's mountain.

They came to another gate-like entrance on the street. Here again, were more flowers, climbing flowers, and walls of gold that they had not seen before!

As they neared it, they heard singing! Once inside, the area was very open and level. Many saints were about in prayer.

Up and above the area, there was a beautiful waterfall.

"Look!" said Felicia, "Look at it, looks like the water is all light!"

It was high up above, but away from the area of this vast sanctuary.

"Felicia, this is a sanctuary, here." said Wee Angel.

The waterfall was water, yet the glories, made the water look like rays, that slowly flowed over the falls to the stream below. To the sides were flowers and the sides of God's holy mountain, were very golden in appearance. There were golden hues of light and color coming from it!

The sanctuary was molded into the sides of God's mountain.

Around the sides were several sections with many children in a choir. Many, children sang songs of glory or praise!

Also at higher levels were little angels singing! Of course, they were just a little bigger than Wee Angel. It seems Wee Angel was always a little smaller than the other angels.

"Must be a reason. I'm always smaller in size." spoke Wee Angel as she was describing the scene to Felicia.

"What beautiful singing!" added Felicia.. The mountain rang with these beautiful voices, singing glories to God. All the angels and saints, after a song, would praise and sing praises to God there and above.

There was a special children's orchestra and also some angels in it.

Above, the angels hovered in the glories, and along the mountainsides were also angels with instruments. They also were above the entrance.

The falls with the waters like light was very wide and awesome! It was wide and looked like it came right out of the holy mountain in pure light. All was pure and very holy.

The scene was beautiful, the sounds were awesome, the praises were mighty at times, with trumpets blowing! The violinists played in unison.

All to glorify the great Creator above them, and amidst them.

Felicia was so overwhelmed and so joyful, that she bubbled with excitement. Both were all smiles, ear to ear, yet their little heavenly hearts were filled with awesome feelings at the singing. There were rows and rows of standing children, all along the sides.

There were divided parts of God's mountain that made different sections to the sanctuary as was molded together for them in appearance. The mountain was glowing! Saints and angels came and went to this as the singing continued for everyone.

The two walked back through the entrance.

They talked with several children outside the entrance. There were seven children. They were Grant, James, Wayne, Mike, Brittany, Cindy and Laura.

There were many children headed to this sanctuary.

Back on the street, angels flew about on their way.

Many saints walked, and those with wings flew above the streets.

Wee Angel and Felicia still talked with the children.

Finally, Brittany said, "Can we pray with you, Wee Angel and Felicia?"

They gathered together and Brittany led the prayer. "Thank you, God for little Wee Angel and Felicia and us, children. Thank you that we can be here. We praise you and we love you!"

They visited for quite a heavenly time. They expressed their joys of heaven!

Some white doves flew about them. The white doves were always a beautiful sight around the Lord's city. Beautiful like the Holy Spirit, God's Dove!

They said their good days and Wee Angel with Felicia walked on, while the children went into the sanctuary.

Daniel Leske

Chapter 17

The Throne Room

So much was about them in the beauty of God's city.

Wee Angel said, "Felicia, we are going to go to some higher mansions on this mountain in this city!

"That sounds great!" said Felicia.

So on they went walking upwards, and at times, they flew along to the golden way and even up the stairways. They were often in the open so one could see the gem mansions, rivers, and falls.

As they went upward from where they were, they saw part of the service and choirs. They saw the falls above again!

The service had many glories above and around it.

So upward they went, then into a special mansion on the mountainside. This mansion had many gems.

Then they flew upwards to another mansion.

In these places they visited were always steps and stairways, some wide and long, others narrow or short. Some were with many, and others few.

Waters flowed and were apart of this holy mountain.

There were gem mansions, courtyards, open view areas, tree areas, flowered areas, bushes with flowers, golden special gem areas, special gems, special walkways, all a part of it!

This was just one area of the city. Other areas around this holy mountain had similar scenes, yet different and always much to see around them.

It was celestial with the gems and the stairways, with openness and yet God created it's beauty with the flowers, trees, waters, and waterfalls, and streams. Celestial in that light could pass through these!

It provided for everyone, those with wings and those without wings.

"We are seeing so much!" said Felicia, "God made this city so beautiful with his mountain."

Wee Angel nodded.

Both traveled about this city and an angel was long the street. He saw Wee Angel and Felicia. He flew closer and flew right up to them. His name was Angel Micah. So they went with him upwards and upwards to see God.

Wee Angel and Felicia stood and waited to see Lord God.

As he was Spirit, they saw all around him tremendous light. There was also tremendous light above him.

They knew the throne was there. The light was so strong they could only see a little of it through this light. They could only see some of his likeness.

Lord God said, "Come, just a little closer."

They walked on and knelt before him.

In seeing him again, in Light and Spirit.

As before he said, "I want to give both of you, hugs!"

The Light moved closer and they were up! Wee Angel and Felicia saw his hands and arms amidst this light. Then he was soon back on the throne.

He asked Wee Angel, "How is it going, my special little angel. I thought of both of you and your travels about heaven."

They answered together, "It's so beautiful, God. It's just, awesome and wonderful!"

The presence of his holiness was always there! The love was there."

He was and is voice! He was and is light as he so stated! His throne had colors around it. The floor like a glass of clear crystal.

Above the throne, high above, wide circles of light with fire went circular in motion. They were like rings of light and fire. One ring would be going one direction, then the next the other direction. There were several rings like this high above the throne.

From the rings of fire and light, there were evenly spaced beams of light that radiated away in a circular motion. Then to the sides were clouds of light with colors of the rainbows about! The rings were awesomely beautiful!

Above the rings, up and away, the throne room had a likeness of the firmament. There was tremendous power at peace, but present.

It was as one was a part of the throne room, yet molded into the very heavens of stars, light, and thunder that he is!

The rainbows appeared high above and they appeared around the throne. To the sides of the throne were cherubims. They were what they were! Their wings glistened with firelight light. They were so beautiful, they were so much a part of the Lord's holiness. They continuously praised the Father. They were a part of this throne area. Their wings moved upward slowly and they spoke hallelujahs and praises!

Both watched and listened to them.

Because of the strength of the light, they couldn't see everything.

Around were glories of light. Angels also hovered and spoke praises!

Lord said, "Children, I'm so pleased with you! I love you."

Wee Angel and Felicia said, "We love you too!"

Again the Light with the voice moved closer to them and again they saw his hands and arms as he lifted them and gave them another hug!

"My little ones, go, now out the New Jerusalem gate. There is a special greeting for both of you. They are waiting there for you. Then go and see more!" God said.

They saw a smile as he said, "Go, I'll see you again!"

"Angel Micah, take them to the street, so they can walk or fly to the gate." Lord God added.

"I will!" answered Angel Micah as he bowed to the Lord and both Wee Angel and Felicia knelt before him. They arose and they were on their way.

Chapter 18

Back With Friendship

Angel Micah walked and talked with Wee Angel and Felicia until they were close to the gate.

He gave them both hugs and good days. They said a quick prayer and he was on his way back up to his duties for God.

Wee Angel and Felicia saw the gate ahead of them. Again where they walked, it was awesome!

There were falls by them. They were high, very high up as well as high on the sides. They were now past any of the gem mansions. They were headed away from God's mountain with some hills about them. The golden street was as beautiful, the glories above were so beautiful!

They looked ahead to the archway of this entrance. To the sides were walls of gems.

Wee Angel said, "This gate is called the New Jerusalem gate to God's city.

Felicia looked at the walls and expressed her joy of them, "Wee Angel, God does everything just right. Here we just saw him, visited him, and now we are headed through a special gate.

Wee Angel said, "Felicia, I wanted to share a little with you. The cherubim have more wings on them because they are a part of praising God."

She went on, "Lord God said one time that he has his feet upon earth. The throne room's floor is glass-like so he can see earth from the throne when he wants too!"

"Wee Angel, I know that I know he cares so much! Thank you for sharing that with me."

Both stood again in awe of everything around them which included, the walls, the gate, the waters, all the bushes, and the hedges with flowers along the golden street. Also in the distance, away from the street and along the wall, were some mansions. The wall seemed like it was molded with the hills and terrain. There were some streams that ran by it for a short distance from a falls.

As they looked back at the city, it was all glories! Beautiful colors above, as one looked upward into God's mountain, that went above everything.

And as before with the glories, they could not see the peak. It went upward and into the glories of light in the distance, with the city between God's mountain, and the wall.

The terrain was very level, with gentle hills.

The gate was pearl-like with light. It had streams of light around it.

"It so beautiful!" Felicia kept saying, "That's all I can say!"

Wee Angel looked at Felicia and yet knew what she meant!"

They walked through the gate that left God's city. The experience was awesome and both were happy, exuberant. They walked away from the gate, then they looked ahead, saw some trees, some grazing grounds with beautiful flowers, and gardened areas about it.

"Look!" Wee Angel said, "Felicia, look!"

Felicia looked and saw what Wee Angel was saying!

"It's Sir William and Tuddley Teddy, together for us. That's what God meant, something special!"

Both flew and winged next to them. One hugged Sir William, and the other hugged Tuddley Teddy. Wee Angel and Felicia danced about, flew around them, and played with them. Sir William and Tuddley Teddy ran about as well in the excitement of the two.

Wee Angel said to Felicia, "God said that I should take you to more places, so that's what we are going to do!"

Wee Angel and Felicia stood by them.

They prayed and Felicia rubbed the tears from her watered eyes over this joy. She was so happy! Wee Angel was so happy too!

Tuddley Teddy and Sir William were also happy! They were happy to be friends and they were happy to be a part of this joy of heaven!

Daniel Leske is available for speaking engagements and public appearances. For more information contact:

Daniel Leske
C/O Advantage Books
P.O. Box 160847
Altamonte Springs, FL 32716

info@ advbooks.com

Daniel has also published *The Joy of Heaven 1* and *The Joy of Heaven 3* available from *Advantage Books*

To purchase additional copies of this book or other books published by *Advantage Books* call our order number at:

407-788-3110 (Book Orders Only)

or visit our bookstore website at: www.advbookstore.com

We are planning to have some children's products of the characters from *The Joy of Heaven 1, 2,* and *3*. They would be stuffed animal toys, teddy bears, figurines, possibly dolls and other products. For more information:

www.thejoyofheaven.com

Facebook: Daniel Leske / Author

*A*dvantage
BOOKS

Longwood, Florida, USA
"we bring dreams to life"™
www.advbookstore.com

www.ingramcontent.com/pod-product-compliance
Lightning Source LLC
Chambersburg PA
CBHW081520040426
42447CB00013B/3279

* 9 7 8 1 5 9 7 5 5 2 4 2 4 *